Livewire

REAL LIVES

Teacher's
Resource Book

JAMESTOWN PUBLISHERS

a division of NTC/CONTEMPORARY PUBLISHING GROUP
Lincolnwood, Illinois USA

ISBN: 0-8092-9545-8

Published by Jamestown Publishers,
a division of NTC/Contemporary Publishing Group, Inc.
4255 West Touhy Avenue,
Lincolnwood (Chicago), Illinois 60712-1975
© 2001 by NTC/Contemporary Publishing Group, Inc.

01 02 03 04 05 06 MP 10 9 8 7 6 5 4 3 2 1

CONTENTS

ABOUT THE *LIVEWIRE REAL LIVES* SERIES

Livewire Real Lives is a series of 25 biographies for struggling teenage and adult readers looking for enjoyable but challenging material that improves their reading skills. The series features high-interest biographies of famous people from history and from the sports and entertainment fields, written at low-level readabilities. Each book sustains the attention of developing readers by offering short selections that inspire comments and stimulate discussion. Reluctant readers will be intrigued by the historical figures and celebrities who are subjects of the biographies. The compact size and nontextbook format of the books also add to their appeal.

The *Real Lives* series is perfect for older readers looking for comfortable but engaging materials. The readability levels, size, and format of the books provide opportunities for successful, worthwhile reading experiences. A complete list of the titles and readability levels of books in the series is on page vi. The books are arranged alphabetically by category.

Each book has been carefully planned, with appropriate vocabulary and sentence structure. Line length, line spacing, page layout, and liberal use of photographs also help to make the books approachable. Color bands on the front and back covers indicate the readability level of each book.

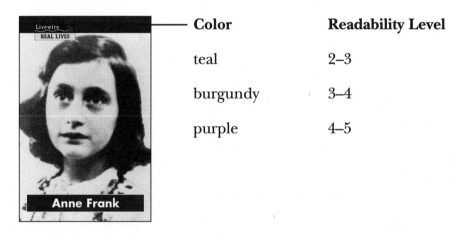

Color	Readability Level
teal	2–3
burgundy	3–4
purple	4–5

This Teacher's Resource Book provides reproducible activity sheets and extension work for all the *Real Lives* books. Reading comprehension is the main focus of the activities. Simple activities such as multiple choice and cause-and-effect exercises prompt students to go beyond the text for reinforcement. The activity sheets also include short writing tasks and exercises in spelling, grammar, and punctuation.

USING THE LIVEWIRE SERIES

1. Preparing to read

Don't rush into reading. Talk with the students first. Or, rather, listen to the students, especially to what they think of their reading abilities—they are experts on their own daily progress. A word of warning! Many students have spent years skillfully concealing their reading difficulties, so it may take you some time to observe their individual problems clearly.

2. Choosing a book

Some students are reluctant readers because they have tried to read materials that are too difficult. Successful reading experiences lead to an increased interest in reading. When you are introducing a student to the *Real Lives* series, it's a good idea to choose a book that you know he or she can read. After that initial experience, allowing students free choice of titles in the series is probably the best policy. Students will be more successful when they make the choices, even if the books they choose are above their usual reading level. Clearly, though, common sense and your own judgment will play an important part in guiding the students.

3. Reading the book

There is a variety of ways to use the *Real Lives* books with students.

- **Prereading**   Access students' prior knowledge by discussing the subject of the biography and the historical period in which he or she lived. You may wish to have students start filling in a KWL Strategy Chart with what they already know about the subject and what they want to know.

- **Individual silent reading**   This approach can be very successful for interested or well-motivated students. You may wish to have the students read silently first, and then read aloud to an adult or a better reader.

- **Paired reading with the teacher**   Even if students are working in groups, it is helpful to spend some time listening to each individual read aloud. You can support the student by joining in the reading of a difficult passage, by discreetly prompting, or by correcting miscues. It is also a good idea to pause every now and then and ask questions about what students have read so far. Or you may ask students to generate questions about what they have read. Volunteer helpers or older students can also provide this support.

- **Paired or group reading with other students**   Paired reading can be very successful when partners are similar in ability or when a student can benefit from hearing a more-fluent reader model good reading. Reading groups should be carefully chosen, flexible, and not too large. Be sure that the students in a group are able to work together comfortably.

USING THE ACTIVITY SHEETS

After a student has read a book, he or she will be ready to complete the activity sheets for that book. The activity sheets include the following:

- basic reading comprehension activities, such as main idea and cause-and-effect exercises
- critical thinking activities that refer to the text and ask for readers' opinions and views
- a spelling activity to be used with any book
- a Reading Response sheet on which students can record their reading histories and respond personally to each book.

Some of these activities will be more effective if completed individually; others may work better through discussion in pairs or small groups. Working on the activity sheets at home is also a good way for students to involve parents or elder brothers or sisters in their reading.

LIVEWIRE REAL LIVES BOOKS

HISTORY	READABILITY LEVEL	ACTIVITY PAGES
Winston Churchill	4–5	1–2
Leonardo da Vinci	4–5	3–4
Diana, Princess of Wales	3–4	5–6
Anne Frank	4–5	7–8
Mahatma Gandhi	4–5	9–10
John F. Kennedy	3–4	11–12
Martin Luther King, Jr.	4–5	13–14
Nelson Mandela	3–4	15–16
Wolfgang Mozart	4–5	17–18
Florence Nightingale	4–5	19–20
Franklin D. Roosevelt	4–5	21–22
Sitting Bull	3–4	23–24
Mother Teresa	3–4	25–26
Vincent van Gogh	3–4	27–28
SPORTS AND ENTERTAINMENT		
Muhammad Ali	2–3	29–30
Tom Cruise	3–4	31–32
Clint Eastwood	3–4	33–34
Mel Gibson	3–4	35–36
Michael Jordan	3–4	37–38
Marilyn Monroe	4–5	39–40
Michelle Pfeiffer	3–4	41–42
Keanu Reeves	3–4	43–44
Arnold Schwarzenegger	4–5	45–46
Will Smith	2–3	47–48
John Travolta	3–4	49–50

WINSTON CHURCHILL

A *cause* is the reason why something happens. An *effect* is what happens. Look at these causes and effects of events in Winston Churchill's life.

1. Underline the **cause**.

   a. Churchill saved a train during the Boer War.
   He was welcomed home as a hero.

   b. Churchill sent guns and money to help the White Russians.
   He was against the Communists they were fighting.

   c. Churchill did not trust Hitler.
   Britain began building up its army, navy, and air force.

   d. The Japanese bombed Pearl Harbor.
   Then the United States entered World War II.

   e. The Allies wanted to end the war.
   Churchill agreed to bomb Dresden.

2. Underline the **effect**.

   a. Churchill was the head of the Board of Trade.
   He helped people find work.

   b. In 1940 the British government fell.
   Then Churchill was asked to be prime minister.

   c. Churchill ordered French battleships destroyed.
   He did not want the Germans to get them.

   d. Churchill resigned as prime minister.
   The Labour Party won the election in 1945.

   e. Churchill was made an honorary U.S. citizen.
   He was a great friend to America.

WINSTON CHURCHILL

Direct quotations help make a biography come alive.
Choose the word that best completes each quotation
by Winston Churchill. Write the word on the line.

1. "We shall never _____." (surrender, fight)

2. "There was never a moment's _____ as to whether
   the atom bomb should be used or not." (discussion, word)

3. "I have nothing to offer, but blood, toil, sweat, and

   _____." (time, tears)

4. "Do not suppose that this is the _____. This is only
   the beginning." (start, end)

5. "Give us the _____, and we will finish the job."
   (medals, tools)

6. "I feel I still have something to offer in the building of a sure and

   lasting _____." (peace, war)

7. "I'd like to come back and wear my _____ at some
   big dinner." (medals, hat)

8. "You do your worst, and we will do our _____."
   (toil, best)

9. "You ask: what is our aim? I can answer in one word:

   _____!" (Victory, Defeat)

10. "This was their _____ hour." (earliest, finest)

LEONARDO DA VINCI

1. Write the answer to each question. Use details from *Leonardo da Vinci* to help you. The page numbers tell you where the information can be found in the book.

   a. Where was Leonardo born? _____ (page 1)

   b. To what city did Leonardo go to learn to be an artist?

      _____ (page 2)

   c. Where was Leonardo's masterpiece *The Last Supper* painted?

      _____ (page 7)

   d. Besides painting, what was da Vinci known for?

      _____ (pages 10–11)

   e. What is the name of Leonardo's famous painting of a woman?

      _____ (page 16)

2. It is important to understand facts when you read. You can form your own opinions based on the facts. Answer these questions by giving your opinions.

   a. The monks were angry. Leonardo took too long to finish their painting. Would this have made you angry? Explain why or why not.

      _____

      _____

      _____

      _____

   b. What was the most important thing Leonardo did? Explain.

      _____

      _____

      _____

      _____

LEONARDO DA VINCI

Words with almost the same meanings are *synonyms*. Write the synonym for the underlined word or words in each sentence.

1. As a child, Leonardo was <u>lively</u>. _____
   (active, shy)

2. Verrocchio helped <u>train</u> Leonardo as an artist. _____
   (paint, prepare)

3. Leonardo made <u>drawings</u> of rocks, plants, and fossils.

   _____ (letters, sketches)

4. Leonardo became <u>well known</u> as an artist. _____
   (famous, good)

5. Leonardo found it <u>hard</u> to get work in Milan. _____
   (easy, difficult)

6. *The Last Supper* is one of Leonardo's <u>masterpieces</u>. _____
   (greatest works, ideas)

7. The painting began to <u>fade</u>. _____
   (lose color, get brighter)

8. Leonardo's notebooks <u>contain</u> designs for a helicopter.

   _____ (hold, name)

9. Leonardo <u>invented</u> a diving suit. _____
   (wore, made)

10. The *Mona Lisa* is a painting of a <u>beautiful</u> woman.

    _____ (pretty, angry)

DIANA, PRINCESS OF WALES

Facts can be proved. Opinions are people's ideas or beliefs.
For each statement below, write *O* if it expresses an opinion
or write *F* if it expresses a fact.

1. _____ She always liked playing with her younger brother.

   _____ Diana had two older sisters, Sarah and Jane.

2. _____ When Diana was 14, she moved to Althorp House.

   _____ The gardens there are the loveliest in England.

3. _____ Diana became a helper in a nursery school.

   _____ Working with children is a fun job.

4. _____ Diana married Prince Charles.

   _____ She was the world's most beautiful bride.

5. _____ Diana was a perfect princess.

   _____ She worked to help homeless people.

6. _____ Everyone liked to read about the Princess of Wales.

   _____ Photographers followed her everywhere.

7. _____ Diana spoke out against land mines.

   _____ All land mines should be banned.

8. _____ No one will ever be as popular as Diana.

   _____ Diana died from injuries from a car accident.

9. _____ People from all walks of life went to Diana's funeral.

   _____ Diana's death shocked the world.

10. _____ Diana's grave is on an island.

    _____ The world is a better place because of Diana.

DIANA, PRINCESS OF WALES

A summary of a biography briefly tells about events in a person's life. Use words from the box to complete the following summary of Diana's life.

nursery	divorce	1961	automobile
school	Earl	Charles	William
Harry	land mines	charity	world

Diana was born in _____. She was the daughter of
              a

_____ Spencer. She and her brother lived with her
    b

father after her parents' _____. When she was older,
            c

Diana went to _____ in Switzerland. Later she worked
       d

in a _____ school. At the age of 20, she married Prince
    e

_____. They had two children, _____ and
    f   g

_____. The couple were later divorced. Diana became
    h

the most photographed woman in the _____. She did a
                    i

lot of work for _____, especially AIDS, and the effort to
       j

ban _____. She was killed in an _____
      k   l

accident in 1997.

ANNE FRANK

A *cause* makes something happen. An *effect* is what happens.
Read each set of sentences. Write *C* next to the cause and
E next to the effect.

1. _____ The Frank family moved from Germany to Holland.

   _____ The Nazis in Germany made life very hard for Jews.

2. _____ Germans invaded and defeated Holland in May 1940.

   _____ Jews in Holland had to obey Nazi laws after May 1940.

3. _____ The Frank family went into hiding.

   _____ Jews were being taken to labor camps in Germany.

4. _____ Anne pretended her diary was being written to a friend.

   _____ Anne began her diary entries "Dear Kitty."

5. _____ The people in the Franks' hiding place quarreled.

   _____ Staying indoors and being quiet was difficult.

6. _____ British and American troops landed in France to drive out
   the Germans.

   _____ The Franks had great hope in June 1944.

7. _____ Someone told the Nazis that Jews were hiding in the office
   building.

   _____ The Nazis arrested the Franks and others who were hiding
   in the building.

8. _____ The Nazis were sending Jews to camps in Poland.

   _____ The Frank family was sent to Auschwitz.

9. _____ People who were too old, too young, or too sick to work
   were immediately killed in the camps.

   _____ The Nazis needed people in the camps who could work.

10. _____ Anne had talked about publishing her diary.

    _____ Anne's father published her diary.

NAME _____

Writers use specific details to help communicate main ideas. Read each group of details. Choose the main idea that they support. Write the main idea on the line.

Nazis took away most of the rights of Jewish people.

Anne Frank was an ordinary young girl.

Anne's diary was saved, and many people have read it.

1. Anne made many friends in Holland.

Anne wrote gossip in her diary.

Anne put pictures of movie stars up in her hiding place.

Main Idea: _____

2. Jews in Holland were not allowed to go to swimming pools.

Jews could not go to movies.

Jews could shop only at certain times.

Main Idea: _____

3. Miep Gies found Anne's diary.

Anne's father had it published.

More than 25 million copies of *The Diary of Anne Frank* have been sold.

Main Idea: _____

MAHATMA GANDHI

1. Read each statement about Mahatma Gandhi. Write
   T if a statement is true. Write *F* if a statement is false.

   _____ a. *Mahatma* means "Great Soul."

   _____ b. Gandhi was a millionaire.

   _____ c. Gandhi studied law.

   _____ d. In 1893 he went to South America.

   _____ e. Gandhi wanted Indians in South Africa to have the
   same freedoms as other South Africans.

   _____ f. Gandhi wanted to get the British out of India.

   _____ g. Gandhi lived the simple life of a holy man.

   _____ h. Gandhi didn't eat meat.

   _____ i. Gandhi believed that truth and love always win in the end.

   _____ j. Gandhi believed in the violent overthrow of the government.

   _____ k. Gandhi tried to stop fighting between Muslims and Hindus.

   _____ l. Most Muslims live in Pakistan, and most Hindus live in India.

   _____ m. Gandhi planned to go to Pakistan to prove Muslims and
   Hindus could live together.

   _____ n. Gandhi was killed by an English soldier.

2. Gandhi died in 1948. Why do you think people read
   about his life today?

   _____

   _____

   _____

   _____

MAHATMA GANDHI

1. A time line shows the sequence of events. Look at the dates given. Write events from Gandhi's life on the time line. Some events are given.

   1869—Gandhi is born.

   1888—Gandhi goes to London to study.

   1891— _____

   1893— _____

   1915— _____

   1948—Gandhi is killed. India gains its freedom from Great Britain.

2. Details support main ideas. Read the details from *Mahatma Gandhi*. Put an X in the box next to the main idea they support.

   a. Because of his skin color, Gandhi could not ride in first class on trains in South Africa.

   He could not stay in hotels in South Africa.

   ☐ a. South Africa had rules that treated people differently because of their color.

   ☐ b. South Africa had rules that treated all people the same.

   b. Gandhi made his own clothes.

   Gandhi grew his own food.

   ☐ a. Gandhi enjoyed all the benefits of being rich.

   ☐ b. Gandhi lived a simple life.

JOHN F. KENNEDY

A *cause* is the reason why something happens. An *effect* is what happens. Read each passage. If the underlined part of the passage is a cause, write *C* on the line. If it is an effect, write *E*.

_____ 1. Joe Kennedy thought that the world was a jungle.
He taught his children to fight for what they wanted.

_____ 2. John Kennedy was often ill as a child.
His mother tried to build up his strength.

_____ 3. *PT 109* exploded.
Kennedy and his crew had to swim to land.

_____ 4. Scouts took Kennedy's message to the American base.
Kennedy and his men were rescued.

_____ 5. Kennedy was a war hero.
He won a medal for bravery.

_____ 6. John Kennedy went into politics.
His brother Joe died in a plane crash.

_____ 7. He was popular with Massachusetts voters.
Kennedy was elected to the United States Senate.

_____ 8. People in other countries needed help.
Kennedy started the Peace Corps.

_____ 9. President Kennedy said the United States would bomb
Russian missiles in Cuba.
The Soviets removed their missiles from Cuba.

_____ 10. Kennedy went to Texas on November 22, 1963.
He wanted to win his political enemies to his side.

JOHN F. KENNEDY

1. A possessive noun shows ownership. A plural noun names more than one. Read each sentence. Decide whether the underlined word is a plural or a possessive noun. Write *Plural* or *Possessive* on the line.

   a. <u>John's</u> father was a banker. _____

   b. The <u>Kennedys</u> were a rich family. _____

   c. John's <u>sisters</u> had to fight just as hard as the boys. _____

   d. World War II changed John <u>Kennedy's</u> life. _____

   e. Two crew <u>members</u> died in the explosion. _____

   f. They were lost in Japanese <u>waters</u>. _____

   g. Kennedy tried to keep his <u>crew's</u> spirits up. _____

   h. The <u>scouts</u> took the message to the American base. _____

   i. Joe flew bombing <u>missions</u> for the U.S. Air Force. _____

   j. <u>Joe's</u> plane took off from the south of England. _____

   k. Jack went into politics because of his <u>brother's</u> death. _____

   l. He was the Democratic <u>party's</u> candidate for president. _____

   m. Kennedy won the election by only a few <u>votes</u>. _____

   n. The <u>president's</u> car slowed at the corner on Elm Street. _____

   o. The <u>facts</u> of JFK's death have never been very clear. _____

2. Read pages 22 and 24 again about what happened in Dallas, Texas, on November 22, 1963. Write a summary of the events in your own words.

   _____

   _____

   _____

   _____

MARTIN LUTHER KING, JR.

The details in biographies help you understand people. Complete each of the following statements to provide details about the life of Martin Luther King, Jr. Put an X in the box next to the best answer.

1. Martin Luther King, Jr., won
   - ☐ a. an Oscar.
   - ☐ b. the Nobel Prize.
   - ☐ c. the lottery.

2. King went to divinity school so that he could become a
   - ☐ a. police officer.
   - ☐ b. doctor.
   - ☐ c. minister.

3. King spent his life working for
   - ☐ a. segregation.
   - ☐ b. equal rights.
   - ☐ c. the government.

4. In 1955, to protest segregation and the arrest of Rosa Parks, King led a boycott of
   - ☐ a. trains.
   - ☐ b. buses.
   - ☐ c. airplanes.

5. After King and some students were sentenced to jail for sitting in a whites-only cafe, President Kennedy
   - ☐ a. helped him get released.
   - ☐ b. had his sentence increased.
   - ☐ c. did nothing to help King.

6. In 1963, King spoke to over 200,000 freedom marchers in
   - ☐ a. Washington, D.C.
   - ☐ b. Birmingham, Alabama.
   - ☐ c. Memphis, Tennessee.

MARTIN LUTHER KING, JR.

1. Martin Luther King, Jr., worked to end segregation. Read the following statements. Put an X in the box next to the statements that give examples of segregation.

   ☐ a. In some places it was against the law for black people and white people to play cards together.

   ☐ b. After the boycott, black people could sit on any bus seat.

   ☐ c. King could not use the same parks, theaters, or libraries as white people.

   ☐ d. His house was bombed.

   ☐ e. His family lived in an area for black people only.

2. Choose the term that completes each of the following quotations from *Martin Luther King, Jr.* Write it in the blank.

   a. "We seek the freedom in 1963 _____ us in 1863."

      given   promised   forbidden

   b. "I have a _____ that one day, sons of slaves and sons of slave owners will be able to sit down together at the table of brotherhood."

      desire   belief   dream

   c. "Free at last, free at last. Thank God Almighty, we are

      _____ at last."

      safe   happy   free

3. Compare the third quotation from item 2 (above) with the words on King's gravestone. See page 19 in the book. How are the two different?

   _____

   _____

   _____

   _____

NELSON MANDELA

1. Match each term from *Nelson Mandela* to its meaning or description.

Terms

_____	Johannesburg	a. prison where Mandela was held
_____	apartheid	b. system for keeping the races apart
_____	African National Congress	c. city where Mandela studied law
_____	Amandla	d. group of black South Africans working for their rights
_____	Robben Island	e. African word meaning "freedom"

2. These people played important roles in Mandela's life. Match each person with his description.

People

_____	Oliver Tambo	a. South African president who released Mandela from prison
_____	P. W. Botha	b. friend who was sent to prison with Mandela
_____	F. W. de Klerk	c. name Mandela took when he was in hiding
_____	David Motsamai	d. South African president who won the Nobel Peace Prize with Mandela
_____	Walter Sisulu	e. Mandela's law partner who spent 30 years in exile

NELSON MANDELA

A *cause* is the reason why something happens. An *effect* is what happens. Look at these causes and effects of events in Nelson Mandela's life.

1. Underline the **cause**.

   a. The South African government banned mass meetings.
      The ANC met in private homes and talked to members at work.

   b. Money and arms were obtained from other countries.
      The ANC had no money to fund its work.

   c. After the 1960 protest march, Mandela and others stepped up the action and burned their passes.
      Mandela was arrested.

   d. Mandela moved around by disguising himself.
      Mandela was not allowed to leave his home.

2. Underline the **effect**.

   a. Robben Island was the worst prison in South Africa.
      Mandela stood up for the rights of prisoners, and some changes were made.

   b. People from all over the world worked to free Mandela.
      Mandela was imprisoned for 27 years.

   c. With F. W. de Klerk's help, Mandela got rid of apartheid.
      Mandela and de Klerk shared the Nobel Peace Prize.

   d. Nelson Mandela became South Africa's first black president.
      The 1994 election was open to black voters for the first time.

WOLFGANG MOZART

Sometimes information is not directly stated in a book.
Then you *infer*, or figure out, what is most likely true based
on the facts. Read each set of facts from *Wolfgang Mozart*.
Put an X in the box next to the correct inference.

1. At the age of four, Mozart could play tunes on the clavier.

   Mozart wrote a perfect minuet when he was six.

   Mozart became a popular touring musician at the age of six.

   Inference:

   ☐ a. Mozart showed musical talent at a very young age.

   ☐ b. As a child, Mozart had no interest in music.

2. Mozart's father was a talented musician.

   Mozart's sister was a talented musician.

   Inference:

   ☐ a. Mozart was the only member of his family to have musical talent.

   ☐ b. Mozart came from a family that was talented in music.

3. Mozart's mother gave birth to seven children, but only
   two lived.

   Mozart's wife gave birth to seven children, but only two lived.

   Inference:

   ☐ a. Few children grew to adulthood during Mozart's time.

   ☐ b. Every family lost five children to sickness during Mozart's time.

4. Mozart's operas *The Marriage of Figaro* and *Don Giovanni*
   were great successes.

   The emperor made Mozart court composer in Vienna. Mozart
   wrote the music for the operas. Lorenzo da Ponte wrote the words.

   Inference:

   ☐ a. Mozart did not work with other people when he wrote music.

   ☐ b. Mozart was a successful composer.

NAME _____

WOLFGANG MOZART

A biography is the story of a person's life. The biography
of Wolfgang Mozart tells about his work and the people
in his life.

1. Match each title to the correct description.

Compositions

_____ *The Magic Flute*   a. Mozart's last composition

_____ a minuet   b. a comic opera written for
                                       the emperor of Austria

_____ *Don Giovanni*   c. Mozart's last opera

_____ a requiem   d. an opera that Mozart finished
                                       the night before the first
                                       performance

_____ *The Marriage of Figaro*   e. a composition written by
                                       Mozart when he was six

2. Match each person with her or his description.

People

_____ Lorenzo da Ponte   a. Mozart's wife

_____ Colleredo   b. the partner who wrote
                                       words for Mozart's music

_____ Nannerl   c. Mozart's father

_____ Constanze   d. an Austrian archduke for
                                       whom Mozart worked

_____ Leopold   e. Mozart's sister

FLORENCE NIGHTINGALE

1. Details support the main idea. They help you understand what you read. Put an X in the box next to the best answer.

   a. Florence wanted to become a
      - ☐ a. teacher.
      - ☐ b. nurse.
      - ☐ c. painter.

   b. Her trip to a hospital in Germany
      - ☐ a. showed Florence how to perform operations.
      - ☐ b. taught Florence to write letters to important people.
      - ☐ c. gave Florence ideas about making nursing better.

   c. During the Crimean War Florence took a team of nurses to
      - ☐ a. London, England.
      - ☐ b. Scutari, Turkey.
      - ☐ c. Rome, Italy.

   d. Florence was called the Lady with the Lamp because she
      - ☐ a. set up a home for sick women.
      - ☐ b. walked the hospital wards at night.
      - ☐ c. wrote a report on the Crimean War.

   e. The Florence Nightingale Fund was used to
      - ☐ a. build new hospitals.
      - ☐ b. provide homes for British soldiers.
      - ☐ c. start a training school for nurses.

2. Think about hospitals in Florence Nightingale's time and hospitals today. Write a paragraph about how hospitals have changed. Use details to support your ideas.

   _____

   _____

   _____

   _____

   _____

FLORENCE NIGHTINGALE

1. Draw lines to make sentences that tell about Florence Nightingale. The first one has been done for you.

   a. In 1851 Florence went back to the hospital   for three months.

   b. She worked there   until late at night.

   c. Florence worked from 5 A.M.   in Germany.

   d. Florence was happy because   about making nursing better.

   e. She got her own ideas   she was able to help doctors and patients.

   f. Florence went to see   to help soldiers.

   g. She went because it was a chance   the queen.

   h. Florence talked to the queen   about change.

   i. Florence wanted to make   army hospitals better.

2. Nouns are the names of people, places, or things. Underline all the nouns in the following sentences.

   a. Florence Nightingale wanted to be a nurse.

   b. Her family was shocked.

   c. Nursing was not a job for a lady.

   d. Hospitals were dirty and crowded.

   e. There was dried blood on the floors and walls.

   f. A hospital was the last place a lady would visit.

   g. Florence visited a clean hospital in Germany.

   h. Soon there were more towels, shirts, brushes, combs, kettles, pans, and spoons.

FRANKLIN D. ROOSEVELT

1. Read each statement about Franklin Roosevelt. Write
   T if a statement is true. Write *F* if a statement is false.

   _____ a. Roosevelt lost the use of his legs as a result of having
   the flu.

   _____ b. He was elected governor of Maine in 1928.

   _____ c. He was the head of the March of Dimes.

   _____ d. Roosevelt was elected president four times.

   _____ e. The New Deal helped only wealthy people.

   _____ f. Roosevelt felt that America should stay out of Europe's
   business.

   _____ g. He refused to help Britain and France fight Germany.

   _____ h. Roosevelt, Churchill, and Hitler were the Big Three.

   _____ i. Roosevelt wanted to have another world war.

   _____ j. Roosevelt did not live to see the end of World War II.

2. Write the answers to these questions. The page numbers
   will help you find the information.

   a. How did the stock market crash in October 1929
   affect people in the United States? (pages 6–7)

   _____

   _____

   _____

   _____

   _____

   b. What was Roosevelt's New Deal? (pages 10–11)

   _____

   _____

   _____

FRANKLIN D. ROOSEVELT

1. Sequence is the order in which things happen. In each set, number the events from Roosevelt's life to show the order in which they happened.

   Set A

   _____ Franklin married Eleanor Roosevelt.

   _____ Franklin D. Roosevelt was born in 1882.

   _____ Roosevelt trained to be a lawyer.

   _____ Doctors discovered Franklin had polio.

   _____ The stock market crashed.

   Set B

   _____ Roosevelt gave a speech to Congress declaring war on Japan.

   _____ Roosevelt died a few weeks before the war ended.

   _____ Roosevelt met with Winston Churchill and Joseph Stalin.

   _____ Roosevelt and Churchill signed the Atlantic Charter.

   _____ Roosevelt promised a New Deal.

2. Read each sentence or group of sentences. Then read how to change the sentence. Write the new sentence.

   a. Franklin loved nature. He loved outdoor sports.
      Combine the two sentences into one.

      _____

   b. Roosevelt told the people that the only thing we have to fear is fear itself.
      Write a direct quotation.

      _____

   c. Franklin D. Roosevelt was elected president four times.
      Change the sentence to a question.

      _____

SITTING BULL

1. Think about the people and events described in *Sitting Bull*. Match each description to a person, place, thing, or event. Write the correct letter on the line.

_____ Battle of Little Bighorn

_____ Sun Dance

_____ Red Cloud

_____ Sitting Bull

_____ George Armstrong Custer

_____ Sioux

_____ Buffalo Bill

_____ Wounded Knee

_____ Black Hills

_____ Ghost Dance

a. the owner of a Wild West show

b. a group of American Indians

c. fight between Sioux and Cheyenne warriors and U.S. troops

d. a dance some Indians thought would save them

e. an Indian leader in the Battle of Little Bighorn

f. the place where American soldiers killed 170 Sioux

g. the army officer who led U.S. troops in the Battle of Little Bighorn

h. Sioux land where gold was found in 1874

i. a ceremony to prove the bravery of young Sioux men

j. a Sioux leader who agreed to move the Sioux to South Dakota

2. Write the answers to these questions.

a. Describe a tepee.

_____

_____

b. Why was the Battle of Little Bighorn known as Custer's Last Stand?

_____

_____

SITTING BULL

Proper nouns name particular persons, places, or things.
They begin with capital letters. Rewrite each of the following
sentences. Capitalize the proper nouns.

1. The sioux lived on the great plains of north america.

_____

_____

2. When gold was found in montana, miners crossed indian lands.

_____

_____

3. Some of the sioux agreed to settle in south dakota.

_____

_____

4. red cloud moved to a reservation in the black hills.

_____

_____

5. The sioux and cheyenne fought custer and his troops.

_____

_____

6. The Sioux won the battle of little bighorn.

_____

_____

7. kicking bear told sitting bull about the ghost dance.

_____

_____

MOTHER TERESA

Writers use details to support main ideas. Choose a specific detail that supports each main idea from *Mother Teresa*. Put an X in the box next to the supporting detail.

1. Mother Teresa's goodness was clear when she was a child.

   ☐ a. She did not tell on her brother when he stole jam.

   ☐ b. Her father gave money to the poor.

2. The sisters in Mother Teresa's Missionaries of Charity order led a hard life.

   ☐ a. The sisters prayed and worked from 5:30 A.M. until 10:00 P.M.

   ☐ b. The sisters took care of themselves so they would not get sick.

3. The city of Calcutta had many problems.

   ☐ a. Mother Teresa was on good terms with the city's officials.

   ☐ b. People lay in the streets dying.

4. Leprosy is a terrible disease.

   ☐ a. Victims' toes and fingers rotted off.

   ☐ b. Brothers of Charity taught lepers skills.

5. Mother Teresa's work grew fast.

   ☐ a. Mother Teresa owned only three saris.

   ☐ b. In two years, 30 women had joined her order.

6. Mother Teresa had many important friends.

   ☐ a. She could call the President of the United States or the head of the Soviet Union to ask for help.

   ☐ b. Mother Teresa traveled to many countries.

7. Mother Teresa was not interested in material things for herself.

   ☐ a. She gave the cash she raised to the poor.

   ☐ b. She had a pacemaker implanted to regulate her heart.

8. Mother Teresa was given many awards.

   ☐ a. Mother Teresa did not enjoy public life.

   ☐ b. In 1979 she won the Nobel Peace Prize.

MOTHER TERESA

Studying a person's character traits can help you understand that person's life. Each sentence tells something about Mother Teresa. Underline the character trait or traits the sentence shows.

1. Mother Teresa founded the Missionaries of Charity order and soon had 30 women working for her.

   hardworking   skilled as a leader   gentle

2. Mother Teresa canceled the state banquet given for her when she won the Nobel Peace Prize and used the money to feed poor people.

   caring   giving   foolish

3. Mother Teresa opened a school on the top floor of a house and used boxes for tables.

   strong   good at thinking of ways to do things   happy

4. Although she had a pacemaker, Mother Teresa worked well into her eighties.

   tireless   selfish   hardworking

5. Mother Teresa said she heard "an inner command" from God telling her to help the people of Calcutta.

   filled with faith   quiet   wise

6. When the pope gave Mother Teresa a new white car, she used it as a raffle prize.

   foolish   stingy   unselfish

7. Mother Teresa cared for lepers and removed maggots from the face of a patient.

   tender   caring   shy

8. No child was ever turned away from Mother Teresa's orphanages.

   cruel   generous   comforting

9. Mother Teresa set up homes for the dying.

   kind   proud   helpless

10. Mother Teresa used the publicity from receiving the Nobel Peace Prize to get help for the poor.

    greedy   rich   good at getting help

NAME _____

VINCENT VAN GOGH

Read each statement about Vincent van Gogh. Write
T if a statement is true. Write *F* if a statement is false.

_____ 1. When he was 21 years old, Vincent van Gogh worked
as an art dealer.

_____ 2. Vincent worked as a teacher in England.

_____ 3. The church sent Vincent to work with poor miners in
Belgium.

_____ 4. Church officials thought Vincent was a good preacher.

_____ 5. Vincent and his brother Theo were not close to one
another.

_____ 6. Vincent realized that he was meant to be an artist.

_____ 7. Vincent enjoyed painting portraits of wealthy people.

_____ 8. To find peace and quiet, Vincent left Paris and went to
Arles.

_____ 9. Vincent painted because he wanted to make as much
money as possible.

_____ 10. Paul Gauguin thought Vincent was a great painter.

_____ 11. Vincent painted sunflowers to decorate Paul Gauguin's
room.

_____ 12. Vincent was successful at every job he ever had.

_____ 13. In 1889 Vincent became mentally ill.

_____ 14. Vincent died of the flu at the age of 37.

_____ 15. Vincent's paintings sold for millions of dollars during
his lifetime.

VINCENT VAN GOGH

The two words in parentheses are *antonyms* —they have
opposite meanings. Choose the word that correctly finishes
each sentence about Vincent van Gogh's life. Write the
word on the line.

1. Vincent van Gogh had many _____ in his early life.
   (successes, failures)

2. When Eugenie married someone else, Vincent felt

   _____. (happy, sad)

3. Vincent was too _____ to read his work aloud in
   class. (shy, bold)

4. Drawing made Vincent feel _____ depressed.
   (more, less)

5. Vincent decided that being an artist was the _____
   job for him. (right, wrong)

6. Vincent didn't want to paint _____ people.
   (poor, rich)

7. Most art dealers said no one would _____ Vincent's
   work. (buy, sell)

8. Impressionists used _____ colors in their paintings.
   (dull, bright)

9. Vincent _____ the impressionists. (liked, disliked)

10. In Paris, Paul Gauguin became Vincent's _____.
    (friend, enemy)

11. Vincent found it _____ to work in Paris. (easy, hard)

12. Vincent went to Arles because it was _____ there.
    (noisy, quiet)

MUHAMMAD ALI

1. The story of Muhammad Ali's life is told in chronological, or time, order. Write the years to complete the time line about his life.

   <u>   1942   </u>   Cassius Clay is born.

   _____   Clay wins his first boxing match.

   _____   Clay wins the gold medal in boxing at the Rome Olympics.

   _____   Clay changes his name to Muhammad Ali.

   <u>   1967   </u>   Ali refuses to join the U.S. Army for religious reasons.

   _____   Ali is allowed to box again.

   _____   Ali wins the heavyweight title from George Foreman.

   _____   Ali wins back the heavyweight title from Leon Spinks.

   _____   Ali retires from boxing.

   <u>   1996   </u>   Ali lights the Olympic flame in Atlanta.

2. Use the time line to answer these questions. Write the correct date on the line.

   _____   a. When did Cassius Clay win his first boxing match?

   _____   b. When did Ali refuse to join the army?

   _____   c. When did Ali win back the heavyweight title from Leon Spinks?

   _____   d. When did Clay change his name to Muhammad Ali?

   _____   e. When did Muhammad Ali retire from boxing?

3. Use information from the time line to figure out the answers to these questions.

   a. How old was Cassius Clay when he won his first boxing match?

   _____

   b. At what age did Ali retire from boxing? _____

29

MUHAMMAD ALI

Adjectives describe nouns and pronouns. Adjectives tell *how many, what kind,* or *which one* about the words they describe. Underline the adjectives in each sentence and circle the words they describe. Sentences may have more than one adjective.

1. Cassius Clay's trainer was a local policeman, Joe Martin.

2. After training for six weeks, he won his first fight.

3. Clay shouted, "I am going to be the greatest fighter ever."

4. In 1960 he won the gold medal at the Olympics.

5. Clay became a professional boxer.

6. Clay won the heavyweight title.

7. Cassius Clay took a new name, Muhammad Ali.

8. He dropped his old name because it was a slave name.

9. Ali said he would not fight in the war because of his religious beliefs.

10. His choice had a big impact on people everywhere.

11. Ali won by a knockout in the eighth round.

12. Ali was the only fighter to win the title three times.

13. It was a good time for Ali to retire.

14. In 1996, Ali lit the Olympic flame in Atlanta.

15. Muhammad Ali helped make boxing a popular sport.

TOM CRUISE

In *Tom Cruise,* you can find details about the movies Tom has been in. He has played lawyers and teenagers. Circle the character he plays in each film.

1. In *Losin' It,* Tom plays
   a. a kid.   b. an adult.   c. a baby.

2. In *The Outsiders,* he plays a
   a. cowboy.   b. greaser.   c. garbage man.

3. In *Risky Business,* he plays a
   a. rich husband.   b. rich boy.   c. poor boy.

4. In *Top Gun,* Tom plays a
   a. pilot.   b. race car driver.   c. athlete.

5. In *The Color of Money,* he plays a
   a. policeman.   b. taxi driver.   c. pool player.

6. In *Rain Man,* he plays a
   a. salesman.   b. weather man.   c. fireman.

7. In *Born on the Fourth of July,* he plays a
   a. rock singer.   b. politician.   c. wounded war veteran.

8. In *A Few Good Men,* he plays a
   a. gun fighter.   b. politician.   c. lawyer.

9. In *The Firm,* he plays a
   a. businessman.   b. football fan.   c. lawyer.

10. In *Interview with the Vampire,* he plays a
    a. business person.   b. rock singer.   c. vampire.

11. In *Mission: Impossible,* he plays a
    a. computer operator.   b. spy.   c. priest.

12. In *Jerry Maquire,* he plays a
    a. police officer.   b. sports agent.   c. football player.

TOM CRUISE

1. Details in the biography *Tom Cruise* give information about the actor's life. Choose a word from the box to correctly complete each sentence. Write the words.

dyslexia	sisters	New York	sports	play

a. Tom Cruise lived with his mother and three _____.

b. Tom had a learning problem called _____.

c. He was very good at _____ until he hurt his knee.

d. Then he got a part in a school _____ and found that he loved acting.

e. When Tom was 17, he went to _____.

Mission	actor	*Taps*	handyman	*Gun*	leading

f. Tom wanted to become an _____.

g. He worked as a _____ to make a living.

h. He got a small part in the movie _____.

i. He was so good the movie people gave him a _____ part.

j. Two of his best films are *Top* _____ and _____ : *Impossible*.

2. Pages 1 and 2 of *Tom Cruise* tell about Tom's dyslexia. Describe what it means to be dyslexic.

_____

_____

_____

_____

CLINT EASTWOOD

Details tell about Clint Eastwood's career. Underline the word or words in parentheses that best complete each sentence. Use the page numbers if you need help.

1. In the 1960s, Clint played The Man with No (Time, Name, Country). (page 1)

2. He was in the TV show *Rawhide* for (two years, five years, seven years). (page 6)

3. Clint likes to (choose, control, pay for) his own movies. (page 7)

4. In some of his most popular movies, Clint played a lawman called (Crazy, Dirty, Violent) Harry. (page 8)

5. Everyone knows his famous line "Make my (day, job easy, dinner)!" (page 10)

6. Clint became (a citizen, judge, mayor) of Carmel, California. (page 13)

7. Clint is very fit. He (plays piano, dances, works out) every morning. (page 16)

8. In 1992 he won an (Oscar, Emmy, Grammy) for Best Director. (page 18)

9. In *In the Line of Fire*, Clint played an agent hired to protect the (economy, president, environment). (page 21)

10. In 1995 Clint starred in *The Bridges of Madison County* with (Jessica Walter, Sondra Locke, Meryl Streep). (page 22)

CLINT EASTWOOD

1. Read each statement about Clint Eastwood. Write *T* if
   the statement is true. Write *F* if the statement is false.

   _____ a. *A Fistful of Dollars* is a spy movie.

   _____ b. Clint joined the navy.

   _____ c. *Rawhide* was a TV show.

   _____ d. *Dirty Harry* is a violent movie.

   _____ e. Clint did not want to go into politics.

   _____ f. Clint won an Oscar in 1992.

   _____ g. *White Hunter, Black Heart* is set in India.

   _____ h. In *A Perfect World*, Clint co-starred with Dennis Quaid.

2. Clint Eastwood has starred in many different kinds of
   movies. What type of movie is each of these? Check
   the right boxes.

	Western	Police	Romance	Comedy	Musical
a. *A Fistful of Dollars*					
b. *For a Few Dollars More*					
c. *The Good, the Bad, and the Ugly*					
d. *Paint Your Wagon*					
e. *Dirty Harry*					
f. *Magnum Force*					
g. *Bird*					
h. *Every Which Way but Loose*					
i. *The Unforgiven*					
j. *The Bridges of Madison County*					

MEL GIBSON

1. Mel Gibson has played varying roles, from a poor farmer to a wealthy businessman. Match the movie with the role Mel plays by drawing a line. One has been done for you.

a. *Mad Max*	a poor farmer
b. *Gallipoli*	an L. A. police officer
c. *Ransom*	an action hero of the future
d. *The Bounty*	a taxi driver
e. *Man Without a Face*	a Scottish hero
f. *The River*	a burn victim
g. *Lethal Weapon*	an ex-drug dealer
h. *Conspiracy Theory*	a business tycoon
i. *Tequila Sunrise*	a mutineer on a ship
j. *Braveheart*	an Australian solider

2. Circle each movie title in the word puzzle.

```
R  L  B  N  I  N  X  V  C  M  A  D  M  A  X  T
W  T  H  E  R  I  V  E  R  U  Y  M  P  Q  W  F
R  T  N  N  E  Z  R  A  N  S  O  M  U  T  T  Y
B  M  A  N  W  I  T  H  O  U  T  A  F  A  C  E
S  D  F  H  T  H  E  B  O  U  N  T  Y  Y  K  L
C  O  N  S  P  I  R  A  C  Y  T  H  E  O  R  Y
A  G  A  L  L  I  P  O  L  I  K  D  F  B  N  M
O  V  L  E  T  H  A  L  W  E  A  P  O  N  J  R
T  E  Q  U  I  L  A  S  U  N  R  I  S  E  B  T
N  B  R  A  V  E  H  E  A  R  T  M  L  K  T  H
```

MEL GIBSON

1. A summary of a biography briefly tells about events in a person's life. Use words from the box to complete the following summary of Mel Gibson's life.

future	children	English	Scottish	movies
people	*Mad*	Australia	Wallace	New York

Mel Gibson is one of 10 _____. He was born in
          a

_____. When he was 10 years old, his family moved to
          b

_____. He played in the movies _____
          c   d

Max and *Braveheart.* There were three *Mad Max* _____.
                                                              e

They are set in the _____. In them Max saves some
                              f

_____ from the bikers. In *Braveheart,* Mel plays
          g

William _____. It's a true story of a _____
                    h   i

rebel who fought against the _____.
                                        j

2. Write about one of Mel Gibson's movies. If you've seen it, tell why you did or didn't like it. If you haven't seen one of Gibson's movies, choose one and tell why you might like to see it.

_____

_____

_____

_____

_____

MICHAEL JORDAN

1. Quotations are one kind of detail used in writing. Match the speaker with his quotation in *Michael Jordan*. One speaker is quoted more than once.

Speakers

a. Jordan's first NBA coach

b. Michael Jordan

c. an opponent in the 1992 Olympic Games

d. Larry Bird

_____ "Maybe it's God disguised as Michael Jordan."

_____ "No one knows how good this kid is going to be."

_____ "I can accept failure. Everyone fails at something. But I can't accept not trying."

_____ "They should just give the United States the gold medal and get it over with."

_____ "I'm living my fantasy."

2. Examples are another kind of detail. Choose the example for each statement. Write it on the line.

He was Sportsman of the Year in 1991.
He worked hard at defense, and he improved his passing skills.
His father was murdered by two robbers.

---

a. Even talented and successful people experience sad events.

_____

b. It takes more than natural talent to succeed in basketball.

_____

c. Michael Jordan won many personal titles during his basketball career.

_____

MICHAEL JORDAN

1. Comparatives and superlatives make comparisons.
   Comparatives, such as *more* and *larger,* compare two
   people or things. Superlatives, such as *most* and *largest,*
   compare more than two people or things. Read each
   sentence from *Michael Jordan.* Tell whether the underlined
   word is a comparative or a superlative. Write *C* for
   comparative or *S* for superlative on the line.

   _____ a. The name helped Nike to become one of the <u>biggest</u>
             gym shoe companies.

   _____ b. He won the <u>Most</u> Valuable Player award many times.

   _____ c. But he was <u>better</u> at basketball.

   _____ d. After Michael went professional, the NBA made <u>bigger</u>
             profits.

   _____ e. <u>More</u> people bought NBA hats, shirts, and other gear.

   _____ f. At 36, he was the <u>oldest</u> player to win the award.

   _____ g. It showed he could still play the game at the <u>highest</u> level.

   _____ h. He outplayed many <u>younger</u> players.

   _____ i. Many people believe that Michael Jordan was the <u>greatest</u>
             player in the history of basketball.

   _____ j. Other star players say he was the <u>best</u>.

2. What has Michael Jordan done to make a difference
   in the lives of young people? (Pages 16 and 17)

   _____

   _____

   _____

   _____

MARILYN MONROE

Marilyn Monroe's life can be summarized by looking at details. Choose the detail that fits each statement. Write the answer on the line.

1. Marilyn was born on June 21, _____.
   1936   1916   1926

2. As a child, Marilyn was very _____.
   happy   unhappy   mean

3. Marilyn's real name was _____.
   Norma Jean   Nina Jane   Nancy Joan

4. Her first husband went to war, and Marilyn worked in a

   _____.
   school   restaurant   factory

5. After her photograph appeared in an army newspaper, she

   became a _____.
   teacher   model   singer

6. She took acting, singing, and _____ lessons.
   dancing   sewing   modeling

7. Her first movie to become a big hit was _____.
   Gentlemen Prefer Blondes   *The Asphalt Jungle*   *The Seven Year Itch*

8. Her second husband was Joe DiMaggio, a _____ star.
   football   basketball   baseball

9. Her third husband was Arthur Miller, a _____.
   director   writer   singer

10. Marilyn died on August 5, _____.
    1956   1962   1965

MARILYN MONROE

1. Sequence shows the order in which events happen.
   Number the events in each set from 1 to 5 to show
   their sequence.

   Set A

   _____ Norma Jean lived in foster homes.

   _____ Jim Dougherty joined the army.

   _____ Norma Jean was born in 1926.

   _____ Norma Jean went to work in a factory.

   _____ Norma Jean married Jim Dougherty.

   Set B

   _____ Marilyn played in *The Asphalt Jungle*.

   _____ Marilyn was in the comedy *Gentlemen Prefer Blondes*.

   _____ Norma Jean worked as a model.

   _____ Norma Jean studied to become an actress.

   _____ Norma Jean changed her name to Marilyn Monroe.

2. How much do you agree or disagree with each statement?
   Mark on the line as shown below.

	Agree	Disagree

   a. Marilyn was very lonely.

   b. Marilyn was a great actress.

   c. She was a hard worker.

   d. Marilyn wanted to be liked.

MICHELLE PFEIFFER

1. Read each statement about Michelle Pfeiffer. Write *T* if the statement is true. Write *F* if the statement is false.

_____ a. Michelle started her career in a beauty contest.

_____ b. Before acting, Michelle worked in a garage.

_____ c. Her first movie was *Grease* 2.

_____ d. In *Scarface*, Michelle played a gangster.

_____ e. Michelle hasn't sung in any movie.

_____ f. Cher starred with her in *The Witches of Eastwick*.

_____ g. Michelle starred in *Silence of the Lambs*.

_____ h. She played a French woman in *Dangerous Liaisons*.

_____ i. In *Batman Returns* Michelle played Catwoman.

_____ j. *The Age of Innocence* was a space film.

_____ k. Michelle doesn't have any children.

2. Here are some movies Michelle Pfeiffer has made. Check the box or boxes that tells what kind of movie each is. Some movies could have more than one check.

	Comedy	Thriller	Horror	Drama	Romance	Musical
a. *The Witches of Eastwick*						
b. *Scarface*						
c. *Into the Night*						
d. *Dangerous Liaisons*						
e. *The Fabulous Baker Boys*						
f. *Russia House*						
g. *Batman Returns*						
h. *The Age of Innocence*						
i. *Wolf*						
j. *Ladyhawk*						
k. *Up Close and Personal*						

MICHELLE PFEIFFER

The crossword puzzle gives details from Michelle Pfeiffer's movies and life. Use the sentence clues to complete the puzzle.

Down

1. *Into the Night* was a _____.

2. *Grease 2* was her first _____.

5. Michelle decided she wanted to be an _____.

6. In *The Fabulous Baker Boys*, Michelle played a jazz _____.

Across

3. Michelle went to _____ when she was twenty years old.

4. *Batman Returns* made Michelle a _____ all over the world.

6. Michelle's first job was in a _____.

7. *The Russia House* was a spy _____.

KEANU REEVES

1. Look at this list of some of Keanu Reeves's movies.
   Check what type of movie each is. Some of them
   may need more than one check.

	Comedy	Thriller	Drama	Romance
a. *Bill and Ted's Excellent Adventure*				
b. *Dangerous Liaisons*				
c. *Point Break*				
d. *Young Blood*				
e. *Dracula*				
f. *Speed*				
g. *River's Edge*				
h. *A Walk in the Clouds*				
i. *Feeling Minnesota*				
j. *Chain Reaction*				

2. For each movie, write the letter of the role Keanu played.

   _____ *Dangerous Liaisons*   a. an FBI agent

   _____ *Point Break*   b. Don John

   _____ *My Own Private Idaho*   c. a young man

   _____ *Much Ado About Nothing*   d. a rich boy

   _____ *Little Buddha*   e. a GI (soldier)

   _____ *Speed*   f. Prince Siddhartha

   _____ *A Walk in the Clouds*   g. a SWAT agent

KEANU REEVES

Write the answer to each question. Use details from *Keanu Reeves* to help you. The page numbers identify where the information can be found in the book.

1. Where and when was Keanu born? _____
   Hawaii   Texas   Lebanon (page 3)

2. What nationality is he? _____
   American   Canadian   Lebanese (page 3)

3. Where does his name come from? _____
   Canada   Lebanon   Hawaii (page 3)

4. What does his name mean? _____
   mixture   the coolness   the director (page 3)

5. When did Keanu move to Los Angeles? _____
   1984   1986   1996 (page 6)

6. What was his first successful movie? _____
   Young Blood   *Young Again*   *River's Edge* (page 7)

7. What was the movie *River's Edge* about? _____
   fishing   murder   pollution (page 7)

8. Which movie about school kids did he make in 1987?

   _____

   Bill and Ted's Excellent Adventure   *Speed*   *Point Break* (page 8)

9. Why was Keanu in the hospital?

   _____

   injuries from a motorbike crash   flu   weakness from weight loss
   (page 10)

10. Which of these events did *not* happen in 1993?

    _____

    Keanu's friend River Phoenix died.   *Speed* became a hit.
    Keanu played in the film *Little Buddha*. (pages 19–20)

ARNOLD SCHWARZENEGGER

1. A time line shows when events happen. Sometimes dates of events are given. Sometimes you can determine the dates by information in the text. Study these events from Arnold Schwarzenegger's life. Complete the time line by writing dates on the lines.

___1947___   Arnold is born in Austria.

_____   Arnold spends a year in the Austrian army.

_____   Arnold comes to America.
                   In the same year, he plays in the movie *Pumping Iron*.

_____   Arnold meets Maria Shriver, his future wife.

_____   Arnold plays in *Conan the Barbarian*.

_____   Arnold becomes an American citizen

_____   Arnold plays in *Commando*.

___1986___   Two years after *Conan the Destroyer*, Arnold makes the movie *The Terminator*.

_____   Arnold stars with Danny DeVito in *Junior*.

[1996]   Arnold makes a 3D Terminator film.

2. Draw lines to match the two parts of each movie title.

    a. *Pumping*   *the Barbarian*

    b. *Total*   *Lies*

    c. *Conan*   *Cop*

    d. *True*   *Iron*

    e. *Kindergarten*   *Recall*

ARNOLD SCHWARZENEGGER

A summary tells a story briefly. Complete the following
summary by filling in the blanks. Use the terms in the box.

future	gyms	second	politics
movie	children	born	career
Planet	builder	third	fourth

Arnold was _____ in Austria. He began his first

a

_____ at age 15. He began training to be a body

b

_____. He became Mr. Universe. When he was 21, Arnold

c

began his _____ career. He got his first part in the

d

_____ *Pumping Iron*. His most popular movie was *The*

e

Terminator. He played a robot that came from the _____.

f

His famous line "I'll be back!" became popular. In 1977 he met Maria

Shriver. They were married nine years later. By 1993 they had three

_____. Arnold began his _____ career as a

g$$h

businessman. He owns a chain of cafes called _____

1

Hollywood. He also owns a chain of _____. Some people

j

think his _____ career will be in _____.

k$$1

WILL SMITH

When you read, you often make generalizations based on the facts. For example, after reading about Will Smith, you could generalize that he is a successful actor. Put an X in the box next to the correct generalization for each set of facts.

1. Will Smith did very well in school.

   Will won a college scholarship.

   ☐ a. Will was well liked at school.

   ☐ b. Will was a good student.

2. DJ Jazzy Jeff and The Fresh Prince sang bubble gum rap.

   They became MTV stars.

   They won a Grammy award for Best Rap Performance.

   ☐ a. Will is a good rap performer.

   ☐ b. Will's music is not very good.

3. Will Smith was a millionaire by the time he was 18.

   Will owed a lot of money in income taxes.

   ☐ a. Will did not spend his money wisely.

   ☐ b. Will earned a lot of money as a young rap star.

4. Will Smith has made successful albums.

   Will has starred in a successful TV series.

   He has made many movies.

   ☐ a. Will is a talented person.

   ☐ b. Will can sing but not act.

5. Will Smith played a con man in the movie *Six Degrees of Separation.*

   Will played an alien fighter in *Independence Day.*

   He also played an alien fighter in *Men in Black.*

   ☐ a. Will has acted only in comedies.

   ☐ b. Will has acted in dramas and in action movies.

WILL SMITH

Enclose titles of songs in quotation marks. Underline, or italicize, titles of books, movies, music albums, and TV shows. Rewrite each sentence about Will Smith. Set the titles off by underlining or enclosing them in quotes.

1. Will Smith starred in a TV show called The Fresh Prince of Bel Air.

   _____

   _____

2. Smith recorded the song Parents Just Don't Understand.

   _____

   _____

3. Smith and his partner won a Grammy for the album He's the DJ, I'm the Rapper.

   _____

   _____

4. A later album by Smith was Big Willie Style.

   _____

   _____

5. Smith played a con man in the movie Six Degrees of Separation.

   _____

   _____

6. One of Will Smith's most popular movies was Independence Day.

   _____

   _____

7. Will Smith recorded the song Men in Black.

   _____

   _____

JOHN TRAVOLTA

The crossword puzzle gives details from John Travolta's life. Use the sentence clues to complete the puzzle.

Down

1. In *Saturday Night Fever,* John played a _____ dancer.

2. In *Broken Arrow,* he played a _____.

3. John Travolta quit school to find work as an _____.

5. The baby in *Look Who's Talking* could _____.

6. *Carrie* was a _____ movie in which John had a small part.

Across

1. As a child, John liked to dress up and tap _____.

4. John put on weight because he ate too much _____.

7. In *Get Shorty,* John played a _____.

JOHN TRAVOLTA

1. Match the events with the dates in each set. Write
   the letter of the event on the line for the date.

   Set A

   _____ 1975   a. During these years John's movies
                            did not make money.

   _____ 1976   b. John played the leader of a street
                            gang in a TV show

   _____ 1977   c. John's mother died from
                            cancer.

   _____ 1978   d. John was king of disco
                            dancing.

   _____ 1980–1988   e. John fell in love with Diana.

   Set B

   _____ 1991   a. *Mad City* was one of three movies
                            John made this year.

   _____ 1992   b. John was a success in the film
                            Pulp Fiction.

   _____ 1994   c. John and Kelly were married in
                            France.

   _____ 1997   d. John played the United States
                            president in *Primary Colors.*

   _____ 1998   e. John and Kelly's son Jett was born.

2. Why do you think John Travolta became an actor?
   Give at least two reasons.

   _____

   _____

   _____

NAME _____

LOOK, SPELL, AND CHECK

Use this Look, Spell, and Check method to help you learn new words.

Write down some words from the book that are new, challenging, or important.

_____

_____

_____

_____

_____

_____

_____

LOOK, SPELL, AND CHECK
1. **Look** at the word.
2. **Say** it out loud.
3. **Cover** it up.
4. **Write** the word.
5. **Check** your spelling.

First Try

_____

_____

_____

_____

_____

_____

Second Try

_____

_____

_____

_____

_____

_____

READING RESPONSE SHEET

Date finished	Name of *Livewire* book	What I thought of the book

LIVEWIRE REAL LIVES ANSWER KEY

WINSTON CHURCHILL
Page 1
Activity Sheet 1
1. Underline these causes.
   a. Churchill saved a train during the Boer War.
   b. He was against the Communists they were fighting.
   c. Churchill did not trust Hitler.
   d. The Japanese bombed Pearl Harbor.
   e. The Allies wanted to end the war.
2. Underline these effects.
   a. He helped people find work.
   b. Then Churchill was asked to be prime minister.
   c. Churchill ordered French battleships destroyed.
   d. Churchill resigned as prime minister.
   e. Churchill was made an honorary U.S. citizen.

Page 2
Activity Sheet 2
1. surrender
2. discussion
3. tears
4. end
5. tools
6. peace
7. medals
8. best
9. Victory
10. finest

LEONARDO DA VINCI
Page 3
Activity Sheet 1
1. a. Vinci, Italy
   b. Florence
   c. in the dining hall of a monastery
   d. his inventions
   e. Mona Lisa
2. Answers will vary

Page 4
Activity Sheet 2
1. active
2. prepare
3. sketches
4. famous
5. difficult
6. greatest works
7. lose color
8. hold
9. made
10. pretty

DIANA PRINCESS OF WALES
Page 5
Activity Sheet 1
1. O, F
2. F, O
3. F, O
4. F, O
5. O, F
6. O, F
7. F, O
8. O, F
9. F, O
10. F, O

Page 6
Activity Sheet 2
a. 1961
b. Earl
c. divorce
d. school
e. nursery
f. Charles
g. William (or Harry)
h. Harry (or William)
i. world
j. charity
k. land mines
l. automobile

ANNE FRANK
Page 7
Activity Sheet 1
1. E, C
2. C, E
3. E, C
4. C, E
5. E, C
6. C, E
7. C, E
8. C, E
9. E, C
10. C, E

Page 8
Activity Sheet 2
1. Anne Frank was an ordinary young girl.
2. Nazis took away most of the rights of Jewish people.
3. Anne's diary was saved, and many people have read it.

MAHATMA GANDHI
Page 9
Activity Sheet 1
1. a. T
   b. F
   c. T
   d. F
   e. T
   f. T
   g. T
   h. T
   i. T
   j. F
   k. T
   l. T
   m. T
   n. F

2. Answers will vary, but should include the concept that Gandhi's method of nonviolent protest was a model for future civil rights leaders, including Martin Luther King, Jr.

Page 10
Activity Sheet 2
1. 1891—Gandhi passes his law exams.
   1893—Gandhi goes to South Africa.
   1915—Gandhi returns to India.
2. a. a   b. b

JOHN F. KENNEDY
Page 11
Activity Sheet 1
1. E
2. C
3. E
4. C
5. E
6. E
7. C
8. C
9. F
10. E

Page 12
Activity Sheet 2
1. a. Possessive
   b. Plural
   c. Plural
   d. Possessive
   e. Plural
   f. Plural
   g. Possessive
   h. Plural
   i. Plural
   j. Possessive
   k. Possessive
   l. Possessive
   m. Plural
   n. Possessive
   o. Plural
2. Answers will vary.

MARTIN LUTHER KING, JR.
Page 13
Activity Sheet 1
1. b
2. c
3. b
4. b
5. a
6. a

Page 14
Activity Sheet 2
1. a   c   e
2. a. promised   c. free
   b. dream
3. The quote on the gravestone says "Free at last, free at last. Thank God Almighty I'm free at last instead of " . . . we are free at last."

NELSON MANDELA

Page 15
Activity Sheet 1
Terms
1. c b d e a

People
2. e a d c b

Page 16
Activity Sheet 2
1. Underline these causes.
   a. The South African government banned mass meetings.
   b. The ANC had no money to fund its work.
   c. After the 1960 protest march, Mandela and others stepped up the action and burned their passes.
   d. Mandela was not allowed to leave his home.
2. Underline these effects.
   a. Mandela stood up for the rights of prisoners, and some changes were made.
   b. People from all over the world worked to free Mandela.
   c. Mandela and de Klerk shared the Nobel Peace Prize.
   d. Nelson Mandela became South Africa's first black president.

WOLFGANG MOZART

Page 17
Activity Sheet 1
1. a   3. a
2. b   4. b

Activity Sheet 2
Page 18
Compositions
1. c e d a b

People
2. b d e a c

FLORENCE NIGHTINGALE

Page 19
Activity Sheet 1
1. a. b   d. b
   b. c   e. c
   c. b
2. Paragraphs will vary.

Page 20
Activity Sheet 2
1. a. In 1851 Florence went back to the hospital in Germany.
   b. She worked there for three months.
   c. Florence worked from 5 A.M. until late at night.
   d. Florence was happy because she was able to help doctors and patients.
   e. She got her own ideas about making nursing better.
   f. Florence went to see the queen.
   g. She went because it was a chance to help soldiers.
   h. Florence talked to the queen about change.
   i. Florence wanted to make the army hospitals better in the future.
2. Underline the following nouns.
   a. Florence Nightingale, nurse
   b. family
   c. Nursing, job, lady
   d. Hospitals
   e. blood, floors, walls
   f. hospital, place, lady
   g. Florence, hospital, Germany
   h. towels, shirts, brushes, combs, kettles, pans, spoons

FRANKLIN D. ROOSEVELT

Page 21
Activity Sheet 1
1. a. F   f. F
   b. F   g. F
   c. T   h. F
   d. T   i. F
   e. F   j. T
2. a. Answers will vary but should include the concepts that people lost money and jobs and that many people became homeless and had to beg for food
   b. Answers will vary but should include the concept that the New Deal was Roosevelt's plan for helping the United States recover from the bad times.

Page 22
Activity Sheet 2
1. Set A   2   1   3   4   5
   Set B   3   5   4   2   1
2. a. Franklin loved nature and outdoor sports.
   b. Roosevelt told the people, "The only thing we have to fear is fear itself."
   c. How many times was Franklin D. Roosevelt elected president?

SITTING BULL

Page 23
Activity Sheet 1
1. c i j e g b a f h d
2. a. A tepee is a cone-shaped tent made from cloth or buffalo skins.
   b. Custer and most of his troops were killed in that battle.

Page 24
Activity Sheet 2
1. The Sioux lived on the Great Plains of North America.
2. When gold was found in Montana, miners crossed Indian lands.
3. Some of the Sioux agreed to settle in South Dakota.
4. Red Cloud moved to a reservation in the Black Hills.
5. The Sioux and Cheyenne fought Custer and his troops.
6. The Sioux won the Battle of Little Bighorn.
7. Kicking Bear told Sitting Bull about the Ghost Dance.

MOTHER TERESA

Page 25
Activity Sheet 1
1. a   5. b
2. a   6. a
3. b   7. a
4. a   8. b

Page 26
Activity Sheet 2
1. skilled as a leader
2. caring, giving
3. good at thinking of ways to do things
4. tireless, hardworking
5. filled with faith
6. unselfish
7. tender, caring
8. generous, comforting
9. kind
10. good at getting help

VINCENT VAN GOGH
Page 27
Activity Sheet 1

1. T	9. F
2. T	10. F
3. T	11. T
4. F	12. F
5. F	13. T
6. T	14. F
7. F	15. F
8. T	

Page 28
Activity Sheet 2

1. failures	7. buy
2. sad	8. bright
3. shy	9. liked
4. less	10. friend
5. right	11. hard
6. rich	12. quiet

MUHAMMAD ALI
Page 29
Activity Sheet 1
1. 1954 Clay wins his first boxing match.
   1960 Clay wins the gold medal in boxing at the Rome Olympics.
   1964 Clay changes his name to Muhammad Ali.
   1970 Ali is allowed to box again.
   1974 Ali wins the heavyweight title from George Foreman.
   1978 Ali wins back the heavyweight title from Leon Spinks.
   1981 Ali retires from boxing.
2. a. 1954   d. 1964
   b. 1967   e. 1981
   c. 1978
3. a. 12   b. 39

Page 30
Activity Sheet 2
1. local (policeman)
2. six (weeks,) first (fight)
3. greatest (fighter)
4. gold (medal)
5. professional (boxer)
6. heavyweight (title)
7. new (name)
8. old (name,) slave (name)
9. religious (beliefs)
10. big (impact)
11. eighth (round)
12. only (fighter,) three (times)
13. good (time)
14. Olympic (flame)
15. popular (sport)

TOM CRUISE
Page 31
Activity Sheet 1

1. a	7. c
2. b	8. c
3. b	9. c
4. a	10. c
5. c	11. b
6. a	12. b

Page 32
Activity Sheet 2
1. a. sisters   f. actor
   b. dyslexia   g. handyman
   c. sports   h. *Taps*
   d. play   i. leading
   e. New York   j. *Gun, Mission*
2. Sample Answer: A person who is dyslexic has trouble reading. The words on the page seem to move as he reads. Letters that look somewhat alike, such as *b* and *d* get mixed up.

CLINT EASTWOOD
Page 33
Activity Sheet 1

1. Name	6. mayor
2. 7 years	7. works out
3. choose	8. Oscar
4. Dirty	9. president
5. day	10. Meryl Streep

Page 34
Activity Sheet 2
1. a. F   e. F
   b. F   f. T
   c. T   g. F
   d. T   h. F

2. a. Western   f. Police
   b. Western   g. Musical
   c. Western   h. Comedy
   d. Musical   i. Western
   e. Police   j. Romance

MEL GIBSON
Page 35
Activity Sheet 1
1. a. an action hero of the future
   b. an Australian solider
   c. a business tycoon
   d. a mutineer on a ship
   e. a burn victim
   f. a poor farmer
   g. an L. A. police officer
   h. a taxi driver
   i. an ex-drug dealer
   j. a Scottish hero
2.

```
R L B N I N X V C M A D M A X T
W T H E R I V E R U Y M P Q W F
R T N N E Z R A N S O M U T T Y
B M A N W I T H O U T A F A C E
S D F H T H E B O U N T Y Y K L
C O N S P I R A C Y T H E O R Y
A G A L L I P O L I K D F B N M
O V L E T H A L W E A P O N J R
T E Q U I L A S U N R I S E B T
N B R A V E H E A R T M L K T H
```

Page 36
Activity Sheet 2
1. a. children   f. future
   b. New York   g. people
   c. Australia   h. Wallace
   d. *Mad*   i. Scottish
   e. movies   j. English
2. Answers will vary.

MICHAEL JORDAN
Page 37
Activity Sheet 1
1. d a b c b
2. a. His father was murdered by two robbers.
   b. He worked hard at defense, and he improved his passing skills.
   c. He was Sportsman of the Year in 1991.

Page 38
Activity Sheet 2
1. a. S   f. S
   b. S   g. S
   c. C   h. C
   d. C   i. S
   e. C   j. S
2. Answers will vary but should include the concepts that Michael Jordan is a good role model for young people and that he gives a lot of money to charity and to train young basketball players.

MARILYN MONROE
Page 39
Activity Sheet 1
1. 1926
2. unhappy
3. Norma Jean
4. factory
5. model
6. dancing
7. *The Asphalt Jungle*
8. baseball
9. writer
10. 1962

Page 40
Activity Sheet 2
1. Set A 2 4 1 5 3
   Set B 4 5 1 2 3
2. Answers will vary.

MICHELLE PFEIFFER
Page 41
Activity Sheet 1
1. a. T   g. F
   b. F   h. T
   c. T   i. T
   d. F   j. F
   e. F   k. F
   f. T
2. a. Comedy, Horror
   b. Drama
   c. Comedy
   d. Drama
   e. Musical
   f. Thriller
   g. Comedy
   h. Romance
   i. Comedy, Thriller
   j. Romance
   k. Romance

Page 42
Activity Sheet 2
Down
1. comedy
2. movie
Across
3. Hollywood
4. star
5. actress
6. singer
6. supermarket
7. thriller

KEANU REEVES
Page 43
Activity Sheet 1
1. a. Comedy   f. Thriller
   b. Drama   g. Drama
   c. Thriller   h. Romance
   d. Comedy   i. Romance
   e. Thriller   j. Thriller
2. c a d b f g e

Page 44
Activity Sheet 2
1. Lebanon
2. Canadian
3. Hawaii
4. the coolness
5. 1986
6. *River's Edge*
7. murder
8. *Bill and Ted's Excellent Adventure*
9. injuries from a motorbike crash
10. Keanu played in the film *Little Buddha*.

ARNOLD SCHWARZENEGGER
Page 45
Activity Sheet 1
1. 1947 Arnold is born in Austria.
   1965 Arnold spends a year in the Austrian army.
   1968 Arnold comes to America.
   1977 Arnold meets Maria Shriver, his future wife.
   1982 Arnold plays in *Conan the Barbarian.*
   1983 Arnold becomes an American citizen
   1985 Arnold plays in *Commando.*
   1986 Arnold makes the movie *The Terminator.*
   1994 Arnold stars with Danny DeVito in *Junior.*

2. a. *Pumping Iron*
   b. *Total Recall*
   c. *Conan the Barbarian*
   d. *True Lies*
   e. *Kindergarten Cop*

Page 46
Activity Sheet 2
a. born   g. children
b. career   h. third
c. builder   i. Planet
d. second   j. gyms
e. movie   k. fourth
f. future   l. politics

WILL SMITH
Page 47
Activity Sheet 1
1. b   4. a
2. a   5. b
3. b

Page 48
Activity Sheet 2
1. The Fresh Prince of Bel Air
2. "Parents Just Don't Understand"
3. He's the DJ, I'm the Rapper
4. Big Willie Style
5. Six Degrees of Separation
6. Independence Day
7. "Men in Black"

JOHN TRAVOLTA
Page 49
Activity Sheet 1
Down
1. disco
2. pilot
3. actor
5. talk
6. horror
Across
1. dance
4. chocolate
7. crook

Page 50
Activity Sheet 2
1. Set A b e d c a
   Set B c e b a d
2. Answers will vary